WALES

COOMBE BOOKS

1901
© 1987 Coombe Books
This edition published 1993
All rights reserved
Printed in Hong Kong
ISBN 0 86283 526 7

The Principality of Wales juts from the west coast of England, separated from the West Country to the south by the Bristol Channel, and with the Isle of Man and, eventually, the Scottish Lowlands to the north.

Linking the Brecon Beacons and Black Mountains in the south with the Snowdonia and Clwydian ranges in the north, the Cambrian Mountains form the backbone of Wales. Here, in the south-east of the principality, the Snowdon Range and the mountains of Merioneth form the highest peaks in Britain south of the Scottish border. Indeed, some of the most impressive scenery in the whole of the British Isles is to be found in Wales: magnificent mountains, cascading waterfalls, winding streams, remote lakes and hills, heather-clad moors and a wild and glorious coastline encompassing rocky shores and broad, sandy beaches.

Wales was always, and remains, a country to stir the imagination; a country of myth and folklore, poetry and song; all products of the mystic quality of the landscape. It comes as no surprise, therefore, to find that South Wales, for instance, is particularly rich in its associations with the fabulous tales of King Arthur and his Knights of the Round Table. One of the central figures in the stories, Merlin, the legendary wizard, is said to have been born in Carmarthen, in the south-east, and it is believed that he cast a spell on an oak tree in Priory Street, declaring that, should the tree ever fall, so would the town. Fanciful? Perhaps. But the rotting stump can be seen even today, supported by iron bands and embedded in concrete! Such is the strength of legend.

Not far from Carmarthen is the picturesque harbour and old town of Laugharne, the home for many years of Dylan Thomas and the model, so it is said, for his now classic radio drama *Under Milk Wood.*

Wales abounds in the unexpected. Here is the smallest house in Britain, and here, too, the longest place-name, virtually unpronounceable to all but the Welsh. The village of Portmerion, inspired by the Italian village of Portofino, and the realisation of a dream by the architect Clough Williams-Ellis, finds itself perfectly at home in its Welsh coastal setting. Here is the Tal-y-Llyn Railway, the oldest steam-hauled, narrow gauge railway in the world; St David's, Britain's smallest cathedral city, and Mynydd Prescelly, where the blocks for the building of Stonehenge were quarried. And so it goes on, always the unexpected, the unusual, and always the mystic, brooding quality of the landscape.

Despite the extensive coal and iron mining that once provided so much employment – albeit with its attendant tragedies and heartaches – for the people of the valleys of Wales, much of the landscape remains unspoilt. Indeed, the clearing of tips and planting of trees around now-disused mines is bringing about the recovery of even this once scarred landscape.

The shores of Wales provide sanctuary for great colonies of seabirds and seals, and inland there are red squirrels, otters, pine marten, deer and wild ponies. There are even herds of white cattle in the north that are said to be descended from Roman cows. The moorlands support a variety of plant life and in the south-west there are exotic flowers that one would only expect to see in a Mediterranean setting.

Whatever the landscape, the monuments, the great cities and the quiet valleys, the real riches of a country are vested in its people. And here Wales is rich indeed. Uniquely talented orators, poets, singers, writers, painters, composers, actors and actresses have been, and continue to be, Wales' gift to the world. The high regard in which the Welsh hold the arts is exemplified in the numerous eisteddfods which are held each year, many of them conducted in the Welsh language and consisting of contests in music and verse. The most famous of these, at Llangollen, now attracts contestants and visitors from all over the world; a virtual Olympics of the arts!

A proud country, Wales. Proud of its language, its traditions, legends and folklore. Proud of its beauty of countryside and shore, certainly. But, above all, proud of its identity and determined to cling to it, whatever the future may bring.

Facing page: the Pass of Llanberis, flanked by the mighty buttress of the Snowdonia Heights.

Left and top: the largest castle in Wales stands in Caerphilly, a Mid-Glamorgan town perhaps more famous for its cheese. Above: the perfectly-concentric castle of Beaumaris on Anglesey, begun in 1295 by Edward I. Facing page: Edward I's massive fortress of Harlech, Gwynedd, begun in 1283. Overleaf: the defences of Pembroke Castle in Dyfed.

Top: 14th-century Carew Castle, Dyfed. Left: the overgrown ruins of Neath Castle, West Glamorgan. Above: Gwrych Castle, near Abergele, Clwyd. Facing page: much restored last century, Castell Coch rises from the trees near Tongwynlais, South Glamorgan. Overleaf: Caerphilly Castle.

Top: a library in Swansea University. Left: the Salon of Erddig, Clwyd, a beautifully-preserve country house. Above: the main building of University College, Cardiff. Facing page top: the wooden shed at Boat House in Laugharne, Dyfed, where the poet Dylan Thomas worked f 16 years. Facing page bottom: Plas Newydd, Anglesey, a fine, classic house designed by James Wyatt in 1800. Overleaf: the city of St David's, with its magnificent 12th-century cathedral.

Top: the strong walls of Picton Castle, Dyfed, which shelter a fine art collection. Right: the gateway of Beaumaris Castle. Above: the shattered remnants of the Norman keep at Coity Castle, Mid Glamorgan. Facing page: the dining room of Penrhyn Castle, a 19th-century edifice. Overleaf: Cardiff City Hall.

Previous pages: Cardiff Arms Park, home of
Welsh rugby. Top and overleaf right: St
David's Cathedral, Dyfed. Left: Talley Abbey,
Dyfed. Above and facing page bottom: founded
in 1131, Tintern Abbey, Gwent, was one of the
richest monasteries in the region. Facing page
top: Valle Crucis Abbey, near Llangollen.
Overleaf: (left) St Asaph Cathedral, Clwyd.

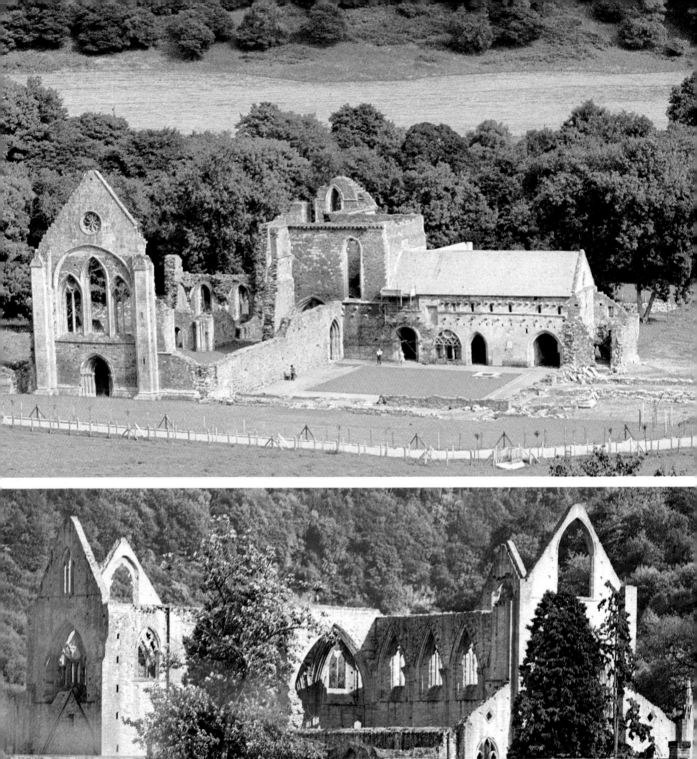

One thousand two hundred years ago most of England came under the sway of King Offa, who built a massive earthwork along his Welsh border. The dyke remains to this day and affords some spectacular views (previous pages) towards Snowdonia. Top: Bird Rock, near Tywyn. Right: the River Dovey at Mallwyd, Gwynedd. Above and facing page: the heights of the Brecon Beacons. Overleaf: Lake Ogwen, Gwynedd.

Previous pages: the Rheidol Valley, Dyfed.
Facing page: (top) the Coracle Carnival at
Cilgerran, Dyfed, and (bottom) Llyn
Gwynant from Hafod Rhisgl, Gwynedd.
Top: sheepdog trials at Newbridge-on-Wye,
Powys. Right: the Brecon cattle market.

Top: one of a series of dams in the Elan Valley of Powys. Left: Llyn Clywedog, a reservoir high above Llandiloes, in Powys. Above: the natural mountain lake of Llyn Llydan, in Gwynedd. Facing page: Llyn Padarn and Llyn Peris from the top of Mount Snowdon. Overleaf: road, rail and river at Ystrad, in the Rhondda.

Top: foxgloves bloom around Solva, a sailing
centre on St Brides Bay. Right: the headland
and beach at Llangranog, Dyfed. Above: a boat
stranded by the tide at Stackpole Quay, Dyfed.
Facing page: Llandudno, the largest seaside
resort in the principality, stands on Gwynedd's
north coast. Its most popular attraction is the
huge crescent of beach, backed by a two-mile-
long promenade.

Facing page: (top) the Mawddach Estuary and
the town of Barmouth, where the National Trust
acquired its first property in 1895, and (bottom)
Llandudno Pier. Top: Traeth Bychan, on
Anglesey. Above: the coast at Rhossili, on the
Gower Peninsula. Right: Whitesands Bay,
Dyfed. Overleaf: Aberystwyth, Dyfed, where the
National Library of Wales preserves many
ancient manuscripts as well as modern works.

Previous pages: Cardiff. Top: South Stack, off
Holy Island, Anglesey. Left: Carreg Ddu,
Gwynedd. Above: Trwyn Yr Wylfa, Gwynedd.
Facing page: Tenby, Dyfed.

The 3,560-foot summit of Snowdon (left) may
reached by footpath (above) or by train (top).
Facing page: Snowdon from the west. Overlea
Gwynedd's Cader Range.

Top: Porthmadog, Gwynedd, whence the Ffestiniog Railway leaves for the mountains. Left: Telford's bridge across the Menai Straits was opened in 1826 and Stephenson's (above) in 1850. Facing page: Portmeirion, Gwynedd, where Sir Clough Williams-Ellis built his dream-like Italianate village.

Top: Gwynedd's Mawddach Estuary, with
Cader Idris beyond. Left: the South Glamorgan
resort of Porthcawl with its tiny Yacht Basin.
Above: Telford's Menai Bridge. Facing page:
(top) Aberystwyth, Dyfed, and (bottom) Conwy,
where the mediaeval walls still encircle the
town and the massive castle dominates the
scene. Overleaf: (left) the River Llugwy at
Betws-y-Coed and (right) the Aber Falls, near
Bangor.

Top: the Shropshire Union Canal winds through the hills near Llangollen, with the ruins of the 8th-century castle Dinas Bran atop the hill beyond. Left: the dam at Claerwen. Above: the tranquil waters of the Wye, from the Whitebrook-Redbrook Bridge. Facing page: cattle graze on the slopes above Llangorse Lake Powys.

Facing page: (top) Tal-y-llyn Lake, Gwynedd, and (bottom) Snowdonia. Top: the River Wye at Llanghope Reach, Gwent. Above: a footbridge in Snowdonia National Park. Right: a stream in the North Wales mountains. Overleaf: the rack-and-pinion railway climbs Mount Snowdon.